The BOOM Effect:

Pivot Point Investors Stock & Swing Trading Guide

JD Boom

ISBN-13: 978-1-7372060-0-2

PIVOT POINT INVESTORS

Pivot Point Investors is a cutting edge company that teaches stock trading at the beginner's, intermediate, and advanced levels. We also teach real estate investing at all levels. Our focus is legacy building and wealth creation for our community and its members. Join us and learn how to pivot to greatness with your finances!!!

Pivot Point
Investors

ACKNOWLEDGEMENTS

I want to take the time to thank God for giving me an opportunity to write this book. A special thank you to my editor, Dr. CeCe Covington. To my parents, Joe & Dot, my siblings, Jessica and Roderick, thanks to each of you for your love and support during this journey.

Thank you Edward, David, Donte, Daryl, Tim, and Travis for your contributions. Your words mean more than I can express. Lastly, I want to thank my Pivot Point Investor partners AC Kash and J-Tech! We did it Gents!

This book is dedicated to JD, AD, ED, & JTD!

Daddy loves you!!!

Table of Contents

FOREWORD

JD has been more than a financial advisor; he's acted more as my partner. When you have professionals, who challenge you to build your own personal knowledge, while also providing excellent investment advice, you can only imagine the benefits. Working with him made me a better investor. The power to help drive your strategies in partnership with JD, is the ultimate framework that every investor desires. JD stands hand in hand with his clients, and always treats your money like it's his. That's the strength and value of a real partnership, with someone who stands as your financial advisor.

David Mitchell
Founder & CEO
Better Outcomes for OUR Kids

Before working with the fantastic JD Boom, I had little to no knowledge of stocks, or how to buy and trade them. Even after becoming more familiar with the process, I still lacked the knowledge necessary of what stocks to buy, as well as when to trade them in order to be successful. All that changed when I decided to give JD Boom's services a try. Not only did I gain a more in-depth understanding of the process, but after following his stock review information, my stock portfolio began to skyrocket. With his 97% overall success rate of profitable picks and his plethora of industry knowledge, I began to make more money. I am happy to have him as my financial consultant and I would recommend his services, every time! Thank you, JD Boom, for helping me to retire and live a more prosperous life.

Daryl Pickett, MBA, CPC, CPMA, CPCO
President & CEO, iCode Academy Inc.
Vice President & COO, iCode Healthcare Solutions LLC.

My occupational career spans over 20 years in real estate and economic development. In that time period, I have witnessed the struggle and plight of financially underserved communities. I have had the privilege to sit with titans of industry and discuss market changing trends. The difference in the two worlds, were not the enthusiasm of people, but simply the access to financial knowledge and the ability to act. In the years I have known JD, I have known him to be a man of passion for serving his community. With years of insurance and wealth management in his arsenal, JD Boom, is moving the needle for the average person to take control of their lives with his commitment to financial empowerment.

Travis Stegall
Entrepreneur

Selfless, humble, and personable are all qualities that come to mind when describing JD. As my older brother, he often served as my saving grace and protector. Being the youngest of three and the only girl, JD always wanted to ensure I was provided for and taken care of. When going off to college, he paved the way by providing a roadmap to success for me in terms of majors and job disciplines. The same premise carried over into my adulthood with JD providing a plan to help increase my personal net worth and wealth by way of solid stock picks, investment strategies, and life insurance policies. I am forever grateful for JD Boom's immense knowledge and depth of expertise. I feel confident that anyone who reads this book will also benefit greatly, learning practical tips and advice that will generate significant additional income.

Jessica Dudley
Entrepreneur

I am so grateful to have a friendship with JD, as he has provided me with intentional financial exposure, which not only benefited my life financially, but also professionally. His guidance helped me take the strategies he shared with me, and align them to my preaching and teaching. Reflecting over my abilities, as a trader, I would consider myself to be a novice trader, at best, but my access to JD Boom instantly makes me a market guru. There is little to nothing that I do in the market, without running it through his filter of exposure, knowledge and expertise. Let me give you this, crown jewel; "We do not have to have all of the answers, information or experience, we just need access to someone who does."

As a minister, I preach the same truth concerning faith... as long as we have access to God, we have access to all that we need. The same applies to our financial trading ability. God has given you similar access that he has given me, in connecting us both to JD Boom. I truly believe that **The Boom Effect** will reverberate through our finances by us applying what we learn in this reading. I don't say this as a matter of faith, I say this as a matter of fact, because I have already experienced, **The Boom Effect.** After your life is transformed from this text, I challenge you to then share what you have learned and been exposed to, with others so that their lives and environments can be transformed.

Edward Long, Jr.
Minister

This book is a short working manual designed to help the beginning Stock/Swing Trader learn and then develop the techniques that will increase their trading knowledge and deliver winning results.

JD Boom has worked with hundreds of people over his 20 years in Banking, Insurance, and the Financial Services Industry. He has helped many clients over the years multiply their investments and has managed millions of dollars throughout his career in Financial Services. He is most proud of helping one of his clients last year, during the pandemic, take $23,000 on March 20, 2020 and grow that into a profit of $118,000 by December 31, 2020.

HISTORICAL CONTEXT: STOCK MARKET

Wall Street: Where the US Market Began

The US stock market began in New York on May 17, 1792 on the corner of Wall Street and Broadway. 24 supply brokers signed the Buttonwood Agreement outside of 68 Wall Street on that day. This laid the foundation for the US stock market we all know today! It is important to know how everything started, as information on the Wall Street/Stock trading is shared.

The very first stock exchange was the Amsterdam Stock Exchange, which introduced continuous trade in the early 17th century. The process of buying and selling Verenigde Oostinische Compagnie (VOC's) shares on the Amsterdam Stock Exchange became the foundation of the world's first formal stock market.

Often times, the stock market, using Bazaar, is described as an outdoor open-air market where entrepreneurs would go and buy and sell items. This includes produce, livestock, fish/seafood, fabric, shoes, drinks, etc.

Tools You Can Use: Key Concepts

- $ **Stock Market:** This is an equity or share market that is made up of buyers and sellers, of stocks, which represent ownership interests or claims on businesses.
- $ **Wall Street:** An 8-block long street in the Financial District of Lower Manhattan in New York City. It is a direct reference to a wall that was erected by Dutch settlers on the southern tip of Manhattan Island in the 17th century.
- $ **Stock Trading:** A person or a company involved in trading equity securities. It involves buying and selling stocks frequently in an attempt to time the market.

- $ **VOCs:** Considered to have been the 1st transnational company in the world. The Dutch East Indian Company was considered the first VOC that set up global trade.
- $ **Stocks:** Equity ownership in a corporation.

INTRODUCTION INTO TRADING: BOOM TERMS

The stock market is a great place for people to make a lot of money, however, for many beginners, all the hustle and bustle of stock trading may cause a lot of confusion, especially if you are not familiar with the many terms and tactics used to win in the game!

Make sure that you familiarize and educate yourself well with stock trading knowledge. You can of course, start off by widening your vocabulary. Here are a few BOOM-terms that you need to know.

Stocks

Stocks are probably the most important and common items traded in the market. These are actual shares of a specific company, which can be publicly traded, with the intent to profit.

Whenever people buy a portion of stock in a particular company, this means that they acquire a share of ownership and investing in that business. Through this, a stockholder is given certain rights towards the company such as a vote in stockholder meetings as well as his or her financial share from the company's earnings.

Stock Market Types:

Bull Market

A bull market is a market that manifests a continuous increase in the value of its stocks as well as a steady growth. Generally, with this type of market, investors gain an optimistic attitude and may want to buy more than sell stocks.

Bear Market

Bear markets mainly characterize significant losses and declines in a particular index or market.

With this type of behavior among stocks, most investors would generally want to sell more of their stocks and may be pessimistic about investing. This type of market usually breeds widespread fear! We will revisit FEAR later.

Dividends (KEY BOOM Term!!!)

Dividends are added or bonus payments given to stockholders after a profitable quarter. With this sum of money, many people may often reinvest on more shares of stock, which allows individuals to earn more money...cha-ching! Think free money for holding this stock! This is also known as passive income. Not all companies pay a dividend. Growth stock companies are an example of this.

Futures (KEY BOOM Term)

Futures, just like stocks, are also traded in the market. However, these are purchased against future costs of commodities. You can earn from these, if in time, the actual price of commodities become higher than what you paid for the futures. On the other hand, you can also lose money if the price becomes lower that what you paid for them initially. There is a lot to consider with Futures trading, though this is not my area of expertise, Jason is our resident expert at Pivot Point Investors. Feel free to visit our site, www.pivotpointinvestors.com, to learn more.

Day Trader (KEY BOOM Term!!!)

A day trader is the person who buys and sells stocks aggressively in one day. Usually, he or she does this several times each day in order to make quite a few small profits within the day. There is a lot to consider with Day-trading, especially taxes.

Swing Trader (Key BOOM Term!!!)

A swing-trader is a person who usually buys and sells a stock within (2-90) days of purchase. Some swing-traders like to sell their position in a stock within 30 days of purchase, and some like to hold stocks up to 180 days before selling their stock position. You could make a case for any stock trade that is bought and sold within an 11 months' time period; this is known as a swing-trade. Once you get to 12 months or longer that is really considered long-term holding stock investing. You are not trading anymore at that point if you are holding significant portions of your stock portfolio for that length of time.

Volatility (Key BOOM Term!!!)

Volatility is commonly defined as the fluctuation of the price of a stock or another investment during a specific time period. The most volatile stocks may experience price fluctuations of up to several hundred percent during the day. In developed markets, volatility tends to occur at lower rates.

Is volatility a good thing for the stock market? Absolutely!!! High volatility means the stock price moves a lot. This price movement provides stock traders the ability to profit off the constant price movement, over a given period of time.

Should You Invest in Volatile Stocks? Yes! You must have a well-developed action plan in which you select the volatile stock, coupled with the appropriate hedge and exit strategy with the specified stock.

Dollar Cost Averaging (Key BOOM Term)

Occurs when an investor purchases more stock as the stock price drops. This makes the trader's average stock purchase price decrease. You may use this strategy if you believe in the company or that the general consensus about the company is wrong. You expect the stock price to rebound for your profit!

Inflation (Key BOOM Term!!!)

The costs of goods and services increasing over time. One of the most important and overlooked facts that affect every investment a trader can or will make.

These terms are only a few of the most used language in stock trading. And upon encountering them, you may certainly have the impression of how intimidating the stock market can be. With the many complicated terminologies and tactics, one can easily get side. **Boom Certified = EXTREMELY IMPORTANT INFORMATION ☺:** Knowledge is key to financial gain.

Remember that if you are new at doing business in this arena, make sure that you take the extra mile to learn more about the associated terms as well as strategies to maximize profit. A little hard work will certainly get you far!

52-Week High (Key BOOM Term!!!)

This represents the highest market price of a given security over a 52-week (or 1 year) period. I always take a look at the 52-week high before I make a new stock purchase.

52-Week Low (Key BOOM Term!!!)

This represents the lowest market price of a given security over a 52-week (or 1 year) period. I usually check the 52-week low before I purchase most stocks, and I use this measure to help gauge what my potential loss or drop in a given stock could be.

Other Stock/Trading Term You Need to Know

Growth Stock Company – A company that does not pay a dividend but offers the potential for stock appreciation.

Trading on Margin

Trading on margin is similar to trading stocks with the use of borrowed money. Using this approach allows you the ability to purchase shares of stock for only a portion of the actual price. The remainder of the cost can be paid upon the actual sale of the stock, or at a later date.

Alpha

Measures the amount that the investment has returned, in relation to the market index or the broad benchmark that it is compared against.

Beta

Measures the volatility of an investment and usually indicates the relative risk of the stock/investment.

Market Close

The New York Stock Exchange (NYSE) and the NASDAQ closes at 4 pm, with after-hours trading continuing until 8pm daily. These times reflect the time when trading ends for the day.

Annual Report

An annual report is prepared by a company to share information on the company. The intent of the report is to impress its current and potential shareholders. It contains a great deal of information about the company, from its cash flow to its management strategy. When you read a company's annual report you are judging the company's solvency (or the degree to which the current assets of a company exceeds the liabilities of that company) and financial situation.

High

Refers to a market milestone in which a stock or index reaches a greater price point than previously. Record highs can signal that a given stock is overbought. There are 30-day highs as well that are more time focused. The high can be a good indicator of the additional and continued growth potential for a particular stock.

Index

A benchmark that is used as a reference marker for traders and portfolio managers. A 10% return may sound good, but if the market index returned 12%, then you didn't do very well. You could have just invested in an index fund and saved time by not trading frequently. Examples are the DOW Jones Industrials and the S&P 500.

Low

The low represents the lowest price point for a stock or index.

Over the Counter (OTC) & Pink Sheets

Refers most commonly to penny stocks, which are traded at $5 per share or less. They are also called OTC because that is how they are traded. These companies are usually smaller companies that are not traded on major exchanges like NYSE or NASDAQ.

Rally

A rapid increase in the price level of a stock, market, or index. It could be classified as a bull rally or a bear rally. In a bear market, a stock's movement that is up by 10% or more, qualifies as a rally.

Sector

A group of stocks that are in the same industry and belong to the same sector. An example of this would the technology sector with companies like Google and Microsoft. One strategy includes traders working in a specific sector due to their knowledge of the industry and their ability to better predict stock prices.

Stock Symbol

A stock symbol is a 1 to 4-character alphabetic root symbol that represents a publicly traded company on a stock exchange.

DIFFERENT RISK TYPES

In this section, the different risks will be addressed. Every good stock trader must consider and master their action plan if they want to invest in the stock and/or bond market, while becoming a successful trader.

Liquidity Risk: a challenge to sell an **investment** or having to sell a share below its fair market value. There could also be high costs to carrying out the sell of low liquidity stock.

Credit Risk: **risk** taken by a bond investor that the bond's issuer will default by failing to pay interest and repaying the principal on schedule.
Treasury **securities** are considered free of **credit risk** since they are backed by the superpower, the U.S. government, to collect taxes to meet its obligations.

Political Risk: addresses **political** decisions made within a country that might result in an unanticipated loss to investors. **Political risk** is among the most important factors facing international **investors**. In many emerging and frontier **markets**, the political situation is affected by more than those influences within the country being considered. Conflicts in the Middle East, Chinese debt problems, American policies and disputes over resources around the globe, directly affect international investment opportunities. *The US vs China with Tik Tok regarding ownership is a great real-world example of political risk.*

Inflation Risk: risk that results from inflation that causes an investor's returns to decline in purchasing power. Bond payments are mostly an inflation risk due to their payouts generally being based on fixed interest rates and an increase in inflation decreases their purchasing power. *This is why money under the mattress or in a shoe box is not good!*

Investment Risk: the probability or likelihood of one incurring a loss relative to a specific investment. Risk is an important component in the assessment of the prospects of an investment. Most people want the least amount of risk with the most possible/probable gain(s) available.

Market Risk: the risk that the value of an investment will decrease due to the entire market decreasing during a particular time period. Market risk is also referred to as "systematic risk" because it relates to factors, such as a recession, that impact the entire market.

HOW TO MASTER BUDGETING AND CONTROLLING YOUR MONEY

The very first decision a beginning trader must make is deciding what their initial stock investment budget will be! That decision could be referred to as "Decision 1a." "Decision 1b" would be creating and starting an Emergency Fund. During this portion of the beginner's course, we will cover Budgeting for Stock Trading, Controlling Your Money, and Why an Emergency Fund is critical to your success.

How much should your first stock trading investment budget be? That is a personal decision but let us take a closer look at the numbers and how they influence stock behavior. How much impact do you want to have? What rate of return are you looking for? These are important questions to consider before you finalize your stock trading budget.

The S&P 500 is a stock market index that measures the performance of the top 500 US companies. The S&P 500 is one of the most commonly followed equity indices. As a reference point, from 1950 to 2020 the Stock Market Index (S&P 500) has had about a 10%+ Rate of Return. This is considered a fairly good rate of return, from any investment, year over year. For example, you could have purchased mutual funds that invested in the S&P 500 or the actual index itself directly and overtime potentially make similar returns without the active work of Day-Trading or Swing-Trading.

I know this is a boring thought for a lot of aspiring stock traders, but the numbers do not lie. The main point I want to emphasize is that it is possible to realize double digit rates of return in the stock market by investing in different types of mutual funds, so your actual trading needs to be at a level that makes sense for you to continue trading. Otherwise, stock trading could be a hobby instead of a vehicle that can be your roadway to financial freedom.

Now let us consider an example of 20% as a Rate of Return which any stock trader would love to have under most circumstances and multiply that percentage by a $500.00 stock trading budget. We get $100.00 once both numbers are multiplied together. Now the trader has a total of $600.00 in his total stock trading bankroll after this trade.

Now most people new to investing would not get excited by making $100.00 from a $500.00 investment; another thing to consider is the entire $500.00 would have to be invested to help generate the opportunity to make the 20% Rate of Return. This is key because you NEVER...EVER want to place your entire stock trading/investment budget into one trade. This is synonymous with placing all your eggs in one basket and hoping everything pans out for you. You are lucky if the stock trade works out for you. In the event you place all of your money in one trade, not only are you gambling at that point, but you would also be overexposing yourself to wiping out your entire investment budget with one (1) trade.

Now let us increase the trading budget to $1,000 and kept that same 20% Rate of Return, and the total amount of profit created now doubles, in this example, to $200 for the same exact amount of work. Your return continues to increase as you increase your trading budget to $10,000 at a 20%, will produce a profit of $2,000, assuming the same trades are used. This highlights the importance of making your beginning budget as high as you can to maximize your potential returns and profits. However, getting into the game wherever you can, is the key! If your opening budget is $100, then start there and learn the stock trading skills that will serve you well once you can increase to $300 or $500. Remember it is not *totally* where you start, but where you end.

Once you start making the money, how do you Control Your Money? How do you become or remain disciplined once you start making money? These are some interesting questions to pose to yourself, but the foundational question is, **What is your personal history or relationship with money?** Are you the first in your neighborhood with the newest shoes, designer handbags, watches, electronics, or cars? Do you eat out at expensive restaurants all the time? Do you have cigarette or alcohol habits that take daily/weekly money away from your potential investing budget? Do you compulsively shop online, while having packages delivered throughout the week instead of investing in Amazon stock? Do you go on 2-4 vacations per year? If these are some of the challenges you have had or currently have, then a mindset shift, coupled with leveraging Technology and Financial Apps will be key for you.

When I look at forming any budget, I always refer back to *The Richest Man In Babylon,* written in 1926 by George Samuel Clason. This text examines finances through parables written over 4,000 years ago that still have validity today! The key character in the book is Arkad and he went from a poor scribe to *The Richest Man In Babylon*. He explained how he changed his narrative through decisions he made.

BEST PLATFORMS FOR YOUR TRADING EXPERIENCE

Once you have mastered planning your investment budget, the next big decision you will have to make as a new investor, is deciding what stock platform to utilize. There are many options available in the marketplace today, but not all the options are best for the beginner's stage of investing.

Whether you are a Day Trader or Swing Trader, the three (3) most important items to consider when picking an investment platform as a beginner are: (1) ease of use, (2) fractional investing availability, and (3) stock selection. Now there are some additional considerations once you progress to the intermediate and advanced trader levels, but these three will give you a solid foundation as a trader.

Here are some platforms that you may or may not already be familiar with. Some common beginner platforms are listed below:

- $ **Robinhood**: Easy to Use and Large Stock Selection Available on Platform, but No Support Tools or Educational Features. (Offers Fractional Share Investing and Crypto currency Trading on The Platform)
- $ **Cash App**: Easy to Use, but No Support Tools or Educational Features; Mostly S&P 500/Large Company Stocks are available, and No Options Feature. There is also a $0.01 fee charged when the stock is sold. (Offers Fractional Share Investing)
- $ **Stockpile**: Easy to Use, Can Use Debit/Credit Cards to Purchase, Can Send Stocks as Gifts/Purchase Gift Cards, but Stock Gains Can Be Considered Difficult to Track Overtime and

site is fee heavy at Stock Purchase and Sell. (Offers Fractional Share Investing)

- $ **E-Trade:** Offers Paper-Trading. A Lot Features and Options are more geared towards Intermediate Traders. Offers Educational and Support Options. (No Fractional Stock Shares Available at this Time)
- $ **TD Ameritrade (Sink or Swim)**: Arguably the Best Platform Available for Beginners. Mix of Education Features/Benefits, No Fees, and Paper-Trading availability with Sink or Swim make this a great overall platform for Beginner Traders to Advanced Traders. (No Fractional Stock Shares Available At this Time)
- $ **Charles Schwab**: Arguably provides the Best Research Tools Available on Any Platform. (Currently Offers $5.00 & Up Fractional Stock Trading)

- $ **Webull**: New Trading App that Offers Superior Research and Analyst Information. No Fees for normal Market Stock Trading. Platform also Supports Crypto currency Trading and High-Level Options Transactions. (No Fractional Stock Shares Available At this Time)
- $ **Stash:** A new Trading App that offers a simple investing platform that allows an investor to focus on individual taxable accounts, retirement accounts, and custodial accounts for children/dependents. This can help you reach whatever financial goals you have. Stash charges no fees for individual taxable account stocks or Exchange-Traded Funds (ETF) investments for over 150 different stocks. The platform charges a $2 per month fee for retirement accounts under $5,000 and $1 per month for retirement accounts over $5,000 with additional smaller fund management percentage fees. I do

not personally use Stash, but the platform has overall good reviews. Their platform users like the educational "Robo Advisor" features as it provides information about stocks, along with the industry specific investment feature for investors that like a specific industry during a specific period of time. (Offers fractional stock investing options)

Boom Certified:

I believe the most import features, when determining your platform, is no fees for basic stock trades during normal trading hours, accessibility to a large variety of stocks and ETFs available, such as IPOs, OTC, ADRs, smaller emerging companies, and fractional share stock investing. You really cannot progress into a top Trader without these essential features. Having the ability to Paper-Trade is nice, but when you have nothing on the line to lose you usually make different decisions and take more risks than you would if you had your OWN MONEY ON THE LINE!!!

Conclusion:

There are a lot of options available in the stock trading platform market. Some platforms like Acorn is too limiting in their stock offering to be placed on this list, but that illustrates the variance available in platform selection. There are several platforms listed for beginners but will be addressed in our Intermediate Trading Course.

HOW TO IDENTIFY THE RIGHT STOCKS TO BUY

The one fun and often challenging thing to do is deciding which stocks to pick for your portfolio. Each stock serves a purpose and should complement other stocks that have been selected for your portfolio. There are so many stocks, industries, and ETFs a beginning trader can choose from, that it can often be overwhelming when attempting to make your selections because no one can own every stock. Trust, there will be many days you may have watched a stock and see it take off for monster gains. You will probably want to kick yourself like I have in the past. Get mentally prepared for that today. There are literally thousands of companies traded on public US stock exchanges as well as OTC, so you will always have an endless supply of stocks to choose from.

Where do you start? When I was a sophomore in college, one of my Economic professors always mentioned investing in what you know and use. Now while that was totally true in that day, this has changed over the years. There are many industries that are emerging like Electronic Vehicles (EV) and Artificial Intelligence (AI) that were not as prevalent back in the 90s, when I was in college, so you have to balance this advice, but let us explore this. What industries are you currently interested in? What products do you use daily? Where do you eat? Where do you shop? What do you wear? What vehicle do you drive? What kind of insurance do you have? What laundry detergent do you use? All of these are questions that can point you to great companies that offer publicly traded stocks for you to invest in. Here are a few examples of companies and their stock ticker symbols for you to consider:

RETAIL/GROCERY/CONSUMER GOODS (All Large Cap)

- Amazon (AMZN) Up 75%
- Walmart (WMT) Up 19%+
- Target (TGT) Up 51%+

FAST FOOD

- McDonalds (MCD) Large Cap* Up 7%+
- Wendy's (WEN) $5B
- Burger King (QSR) Large Cap* Up 19%+

CLOTHING/APPAREL

- NIKE (NKE) Large Cap*Up 38%
- Adidas (ADDYY) Large Cap*Up 9%
- GAP (GPS) $6.6B

VEHICLES/ELECTRONIC VEHICLES (All Large Cap)

- Tesla (TSLA) Up 752%+
- Ford (F) Large Cap-$27B
- General Motors (GM) Up 15%+

Highlighted were four (4) different sectors with competing companies/stocks in each sector. All the companies listed above, except for two are considered

Large Cap companies, and all of the stocks have had positive rate of return percentages in 2020, based on information received through 10.2.2020.

These companies illustrate real examples of Large and Mid-Cap companies that sell goods and services that many of us use each day. I will get more in-depth regarding market capitalization in the next section, but it absolutely fits when discussing how to identify the right stocks as a new trader. Investing in good well-known companies that are in industries that have not been decimated (destroyed or removal of a large percentage) by COVID-19, can nurture your confidence which can propel you as a beginning trader.

Another time-tested place to locate great information about companies and stocks is the Wall Street Journal (WSJ). The WSJ is considered a luxury news and lifestyle magazine now. For decades, this financial publication has offered great information that individual investors have used to their advantage while investing in stocks and other securities. Years ago, a stock investor would not be considered legitimate unless you kept a copy of the WSJ at your home or office. I was first introduced to the WSJ while at college by one of my Economics professors. He said we had to read it each day and chart specific companies' progress throughout each week, month, and quarter. We also stayed up to date on current business/company events like mergers and acquisitions, as well as the companies that were going through a rough time period.

The more I read, the more interesting it became. Once I started working in the Financial Services industry, I would read the WSJ daily, Monday-Saturday. This has been a common practice over the years. Back when I started reading the WSJ it was still in its newspaper form, but today I get the digital version daily/weekly. This tool provides company and industry specific information that can assist in identification of the right stocks to target over the years. After 1-2 reads per month, I can develop a new target list of up to 30 stocks long, and while not all 30 entities are stocks I should invest in, the information helps me refine and decide on exactly what my target stocks will be for short- and long-term planning.

Now that we are in the digital age and our cell phones and mobile devices have become an important part of most of our lives, here's a freebie! This app provides a good source of stock trading information. The website is www.investing.com and the associated app tracks market indices like the DOW Jones, S&P 500, and the Nasdaq, to name a few. It has daily news that is company, country, and world specific. It has a calendar feature that tracks everything that happened or will happen around the world on any given day. The app tells you the top stocks for the day and the stocks that have had a down day as well.

10.2.2020 was National Day in China, The US unemployment rate was released for September 2020, and Manufacturing Payrolls were released. Much of the calendar information could be particularly important when deciding what to purchase, as well as when to hold or sell a specific trade. **Boom Certified:** What is happening in the world influences what happens with your trade.

Additionally, this tool allows you to build your own watch list. I won't go too heavy into the watch list conversation, since that is our next course for beginners, but I will say the app gives you access to thousands of public companies and their stocks. Once you add the stock ticker symbol to your watch list the app automatically sends you information, good or bad, regarding your stock whenever news has occurred. NKE is a stock I heavily tracked in 2020 and as earnings' information was made available, or if the stock rose 10% on a specific day, the app sends me automatic alerts.

BUILDING A STOCK WATCH LIST

There are more than 8,000 US stock exchange issues (available stocks to purchase). That screams an incredible OPPORUNITY for a trader who will put in the work and time to learn the basics and progress from there. Identifying stocks that fully support your investment goals and strategies require several skills, but despite the potential learning curve, this is a worthwhile effort. Building capacity through advanced stock watch lists also creates a trading edge that can carry you from beginner to professional trader, at an accelerated pace.

A well-organized watch list requires understanding of multiple components: modern trading markets, capitalization levels, and investment sectors. A good trader will also learn economic cycles and seasonal factors that can affect each trade on a daily, weekly, monthly, and quarterly basis.

What is Market Capitalization? Market Cap is the total value of all of a company's stock shares. You calculate it by multiplying the price of a stock by the stock's total number of outstanding shares. I am sure you have heard Large Cap, Mid-Cap, and Small Cap stocks before... Well this is where those key terms derived.

$ **Large-Cap Stock**: Applies to corporations with Market Capitalization of $10B Dollars or more (Examples: Apple-AAPL and Coke-KO)

$ **Mid-Cap Stock**: Applies to companies with Market Capitalization of $2B-$10B. They are often used for portfolio diversification purposes and can provide balance and increased stock appreciation. (Examples: Yeti-YETI and Fresh Pet-FRPT)

$ **Small-Cap Stock:** Applies to companies with Market Capitalization of $300M-$2B. Examples: Vaxart (VXRT) and (-Diagnostic (CODX)

Now that we have covered what Market Capitalization is, your main goal with building a stock list is locating and adding as many high-quality companies to your tracking list each day, week, and month as you find them. Notice I did not say good or quality stocks. Why? Well, a publicly traded company is a company, nothing more. When you focus on companies and industries that are making money, and not having its stock price driven up by opportunity, as Day-Traders, you can have consistent gains even trading that type of stock overtime.

Positive and consistent gains now and later as the stock appreciates. I suggest adding companies in all (3) categories to have a balanced portfolio. I also recommend that you follow no more than 3-5 stocks per proposed industry at one time. You do not want to get bogged down with a huge number of stocks. You will be tracking the info within your portfolio and you do not want to miss profitable opportunities because you are overloaded with information. Let us use a sports analogy and compare a good stock watch list to a sports team. You have your starters that you begin the game with, and you have bench players to pull from and insert into the game as it is being played. This is exactly the mindset you, as a beginning trader, should have while constructing and continually modifying your stock watch list.

Here is another place where we can leverage technology and use stock investing apps as well as stock scanners. We will go more in depth and cover scanners in our intermediate course, so you can focus on learning the basics right now. However, this topic or section goes hand in hand with the last section we covered and discussed regarding identification of the right stocks. The watch list is your overflow pool of stocks that you want to watch for a specific time.

Boom Certified: Consider watching preferred stocks for 1 month and once that stock breaks $10 or $20 per share, consider purchasing the stock at that point.

You could also say that you believe the stock is too hot right now and you want to track it for 1 month to see if it can maintain the current price range. There could be any number of reasons why you place certain stocks on your stock watch list.

The last thing you should do is track your progress for your individual watch list as you start to trade them. Track them per category: small-cap, mid-cap, and large-cap stocks. Also track them per industry and season as well. For example: before the end of the 3rd quarter is usually a great time to start tracking publicly traded logistics/transportation/trucking company stocks. Why, you ask? The simple answer is the holiday season: Thanksgiving, Christmas, and

New Year's Eve are all approaching during the last quarter of the calendar year.

Boom Certified To Do List:

- ✓ Complete Stock Watchlist Compilation Exercise on:
    - Robinhood
    - Webull
    - E Trade
    - TD Ameritrade

RISK MANAGEMENT: WHEN TO EXIT A STOCK?

We have now entered the fun zone! Once you identify what stocks to buy, the next question is when do you sell? Knowing when to sell is an art, a special skill developed over time. It is muscle memory that is ever evolving because of market conditions, industry competition, technology advancements, consumer changes, seasonal changes, global trading conditions, and US and global politics, to name a few. One of the main fundamentals to remember when it comes to trading stocks is, it is a not a loss or gain until the stock is sold! I repeat...**Boom Certified:** It is not a loss or gain, for you as a trader, until the stock is sold!!! This point cannot be minimized or overlooked.

Throughout the years as a stock trader/investor, I have experienced both ends of the spectrum regarding this statement. You cannot time the market!

That is another old stock saying that I believe in. I know some of my technical trading buddies may argue that point with me, but in my experience, if you like a company/stock you have to go get it...especially if you believe the company/stock will consistently produce positive results now and into the foreseeable future. This thought process/approach has worked for me and it has also worked against me with several stocks that I have really been a believer in.

Thinking back on times when purchasing a stock as it was going up is Apple (APPL). I purchased and sold APPL several times over the years, but in years past I only focused on the hardware (Computers/Phones/etc.). How could this be? A great juggernaut company like Apple and I trade out of it with consistent buying and selling? One of my stock investing idols is Warren Buffett; he did not like Apple or really any technology company for that matter until recently. His ideas about technology, coupled with my memory of the dot.com bubble collapse, helped reinforce my biases towards Apple and technology in general. The incredible valuations for other technology companies, like Tesla, before they had a profitable quarter did not help either.

There were many times I bought Apple specifically on a green day and used the momentum trading strategy and rode the stock up as it was surging higher. I would Swing-Trade the stock for 3 days or 3 weeks, and still experienced the same result of victory! I cashed out in the green! Sometimes I was up 12%, 15%, 20%, and other times even more! Many of you may ask, why did I sell? I just did not value the stock as a long-term keeper for more than 12 months at a time, until the end of 2019. I would jump in and out of the stock before that time period, and even if the stock turned red and dropped after I purchased it, I would sit tight and not sell, which resulted in a loss. I would wait however many days or weeks usually for the stock to recover and rise above the levels I previously purchased, before I would sell again.

By now many of you may be asking how or when did I decide it was time to sell my APPL stock? Some of my decisions are rooted in historical data. The S&P 500 (Top 500 US stocks) has returned an average rate of return of 10%+ since 1950. With this percentage in mind, I usually do not think about exiting a stock until I have made at least 11%+ from that stock purchase. If you are asking why, the answer is simple... I could have purchased a mutual fund or EFT and helped the stock without doing any trading work and average 10%+ over time without any hands-on trading work.

I believe if I am going to put in work then the numbers must make sense and justify the work. I should not just be in love with the idea of trading stocks. I need to do it where it is profitable in my wallet and the time commitment is reflective of tangible results. As an experienced trader, this is a rule of thumb, but like anything else, if some news comes out about a company/stock, company leader, country, economic condition, or industry, I reserve the right to exit a stock immediately. Even during those times depending on the company/stock I may decide to sit tight and wait for whatever downturn results. Just keep in mind that any rule I mention is a guide, and as you learn more about trading and actually do the trades with real money on the line, the better you will get at making positive stock exits.

Based on my prior statement, many of you may be asking about my feelings towards paper trading? Well, I personally do not like it! I believe the pressure of making or losing money is the drive needed to make sure you are right, more than you are wrong, when trading stocks. This is called pressure! Pressure to perform! Pressure to study companies you are interested in investing in! We are humans after all. You take the pressure out of the equation and we make riskier decisions when we have nothing on the line to lose. It is normal human behavior. Now, I am not saying not to paper trade; however, I am saying that you, even as a beginner, can trade high quality stocks with smaller dollar increments, as you develop your stock trading knowledge and skills to produce a profit.

As I close out this section, I reflect on several times when I purchased a stock and the stock took a dip. I will mention two stocks where that occurred in 2020. One of those stocks was Constellation Brands (STZ) and the other stock was Clorox (CLX). I purchased both stocks during the COVID-19 pandemic at different times. I purchased STZ on May 28, 2020 at a share price of $178.49 and continued to purchase/trade the stock throughout June-July for profit. The stock took a dip August 18, 2020 to $176.44 per share, but I did not panic. Why? Constellation Brands makes popular beer, wine, and liquor. Well-known brands like Corona, Modelo Especial, Funky Buddha, Sveka Vodka, Casa Noble Tequila, High West Whiskey, and several others not mentioned.

Why this stock? Why this industry? We were in the middle of a pandemic, with no end in sight, and people all over the world were consuming more alcohol than ever as a way of coping with our new normal. The stock high went up to $184.87 high in September 2020, but I held on to the stock. The stock dropped to $180. 58 on October 6, 2020; the same day President Trump announced that he was ending talks for a follow-up stimulus package before the November elections and postponing them until after the elections. This statement, alone, caused the entire market to drop. What did I do? Did I sell STZ? No, I still decided to hold. I purchased the company, not the stock! I buy companies.

This company has been around since 1945 and evolved through acquisition and new offerings over the years/decades since they have been in business. My point with this stock discussion is I could have sold it before President Trump made his announcement, but I did not. I was not worried about if I would lose my money. Why? Because I have not lost any real money until I sell the stock! **Boom Certified:** It is not a loss until YOU SELL!!! I was confident that I would enjoy my dividend payments that the stock pays each quarter.

Clorox (CLX) was the other stock I mentioned. COVID-19 caused everybody to run to the grocery stores between February and May of 2020, and everybody bought all the toilet tissue, Lysol, Clorox, and other well-known disinfectants. Most people feared the virus and wanted to clean their homes and offices like never before. Clorox's stock surged for weeks to a 52-week high of $239.87 per share. I had success Swing-Trading the stock at various points between March and early June 2020. On June 22, 2020, I purchased CLX stock for $217.21 per share and I made another purchase of the stock on August 10, 2020, when the stock was at $231.79 per share. Now if you just look at the numbers listed, I could have sold the stock for a profit of almost $8.00 per share, but I held on hoping the stock would break $240.00 for me to sell. Unfortunately, that did not occur, and the stock was being traded at $209.55 per share as of October 6, 2020.

On October 7, 2020, CLX was trading at $215.87 per share. This is another example of, "it is not a loss until you sell!!!" The stock was down for 2 months, and I was still not inclined to sell. I didn't panic. Clorox is a solid company that had a Booming demand for its products. Depending on the time and store you visit today, there are still occurrences where Clorox products, especially their wipes, may still be sold out.

Clorox has been around since 1913, is a trusted company, and sells practical items everyone uses and needs. I will continue to hold the stock until I am able to guarantee positive gains. Trust me I WILL NOT LOSE on this stock and with our PPI training and individualized support, you will develop the same confidence level in your trading abilities.

DEVELOPING A TRADING ROUTINE FOR FINANCIAL GAIN

A good stock trading routine is critical for your success. Now the areas of focus or the things that you might do as a beginning trader may change depending on if you are specializing as a Day Trader or a Swing-Trader. There are a few components that are non-negotiable:

- $ Get Enough Sleep
- $ Pick the days of week that you will trade your stocks
- $ Select the times of day you will trade
- $ Focus on the preset returns you are looking for each stock
- $ Set time each day to read company, stock, analyst information, and general news to

understand the current investing climate. **Boom Certified:** Knowledge is power. Do your homework.

- $ Establish your off/leisure days

Your sleep time and wakeup time are important places to start. This may seem to be obvious, but millions of people in the US suffer with some sort of sleep issue, and as a result, do not get enough rest. If you want to be a legitimate stock trader, you must get enough rest so that you are sharp each day that you trade. There is no way around this. **Boom Certified:** Your attention to detail influences your bottom line, and it starts with taking care of you. Everyone is different and have different bodies that require different amounts of sleep. Get your 4, 6, or 8 hours of rest each night that YOU need and try to stay away from heavy drinking and partying before you trade stocks the next day. **Boom Certified:** Lack of sleep, exhaustion, and hangovers can totally derail a trading day.

Sickness is also an area not usually addressed in stock trading courses. I know several stock traders, who over the years, endured significant losses as a result of being sick, while still placing trades. They took over the counter medication that made them drowsy and masked their symptoms. **Boom Certified:** The bottom line is you need to have a clear mind each day you set out to trade and if for some reason you are not close to 100% you need to wait until you are, to trade your stocks.

Next, pick the days of week you would like to trade between Monday-Friday. I am sure most of you work other jobs and have other responsibilities, so you will have to create a trading schedule that will let you handle all of your existing business, while adding stock trading to your life. In general, I do not like to trade on Mondays or Fridays unless something substantial is going on like a market crash or a large stock market increase. On crash days, I am looking for companies/stocks on sale, and on days when the stock market is soaring, I am looking to make some profits. If neither of these occur, I usually will not make a trade on Monday or Friday of any week. That leaves me Tuesday, Wednesday, and Thursday to make all of my stock trades. You can use this same schedule regardless of the style you trade. You could also pick just one day per week to trade like a couple of stock traders I know. They pick their day based on their schedule and study companies and the market every other day of the week. I could think of several positives and negatives that could occur from utilizing this trading schedule, but it is viable and could serve profitable. However, it is a tight window which leaves you a little margin for error.

Now, we are on to the time of day in which you make your trades; this is where things can get a little tricky. I know a well-known Day Trader that makes all his stock trades in the morning between 9:30am-11:30am. He has a 2-hour window to make all his trades for that day and nothing more. This trading strategy has made him 7 figures and counting. I prefer to trade throughout the day. I see how the market starts and proceed from there. I see how the companies I have already purchased are doing to see if I need to trade those before buying new stocks, and I repeat this throughout the days I Swing-Trade. The key determining factor in whatever time you pick to trade is to stay consistent with what you start and stay disciplined to maximize whenever you trade.

You should have a general idea about what you would like your return percentage to be on each stock you trade. This will help you with exiting the stock once you have purchased it. The more you track where you started and ended each stock trade each day/week/month, the better you will become as a stock trader. This will change a little if you consider whether you are purchasing a growth stock or an income/dividend stock. The growth stocks are easier to read percentage returns with, but income stocks pay monthly or quarterly dividends and the stock price usually stays constant. If the stock does dip, it can sometimes take longer than a growth stock to recover, but you must remember you have the dividend supporting the stock price and your overall returns.

Setting time to read about company, financial, and stock information is what is going to help set you apart from your competition. The more you self-educate on the companies and industries that you are interested in investing in, the better you will perform as a stock trader and the more money you are more likely make. I read about 3 hours of financial information about companies and stocks per day. That is a decent amount of time, but it is small compared to the 8 hours per day Warren Buffett says he reads to stay at the top of his game. As a beginner, you may start with 1 hour a day, 1-2 days per week. It does not matter where you start, but you must start somewhere and take this area serious if you want to be a good stock trader.

Last, set your off days and schedule your leisure time. I cannot stress this enough. If you want to move to the intermediate level, you must do these things to be successful but starting out, they are important areas to develop good habits. How you start something, is usually how you will end it. I take 2 Fridays off per month to just really do whatever I want to. This includes going to the gym, shopping, going for a walk, or just catching up on sleep. I know how my mind works and what my body needs to be successful, so I pre-plan to give myself these breaks that give me the time away that allows me to comeback sharp. I also schedule my off days around holidays, birthdays for me and family, and travel days. The good thing about stock trading is you can travel on weekends and any time after 4:30pm Monday-Friday and still get your trading done. This access opens endless options for you to enjoy some leisure time as well as make money if you choose to.

Depending on where I am going, I do both, but if I am planning on a major party, I leave my laptop because I want to be focused when I trade my hard-earned money. I eat my own medicine with this subject matter, and everything discussed in this section will put you on the path to becoming an outstanding trader.

HOW TO MANAGE GREED & FEAR

This section is the thinking section for beginning Stock Traders. Greed and Fear! Wow... Two words that are the push and pull that every investor, regardless of the type of investment, must manage to be successful. Let us explore Greed first as a topic. What comes to your mind when you think of Greed? Dictionary.com states, greed as the “intense selfish desire for something, especially wealth, power, or food." Everyone can be greedy from time to time. Greed does not have to be negative. There are three (3) areas that a beginning stock trader needs to be aware of regarding greed:

- $ The need for a Goal/Target! (Greed Can Make You Set a Higher Financial Target)

- $ Is the Investment Opportunity Too Good to Be True?
- $ Investment Opportunity Facts vs. Hype

For a beginning trader, having a specific investment goal/target is key to managing your greed and staying on track. If you want to be the best stock trader (Day or Swing-Trading style), you will put your focus and energy on this goal. So, when approached with another opportunity that is not aligned with your goal...FOCUS. Examples include: do you want to invest in my MLM business, hey invest in Forex (foreign currency), look at this crypto currency (that is the new hot thing), or this new Sous-Sous (friend's helping friends) opportunity where you invest $500 and get $4,000 in 30 days or less. These are a few recent examples of how different opportunities can get you off track. The goal is to learn how to trade stocks and being dynamic while doing it.

Let us turn our attention to the "too good to be true" opportunities that will always come along. As I think about this subject, I chuckle because over the years, my partners and I have been presented with all kinds of "cannot miss opportunities." Usually they come from someone you like or trust, and that person probably will likely present that opportunity with passion and excitement. It is easy to get lost in the passion and excitement, especially if you like the person. The main thing to think about if you find yourself in this position, ask yourself, "Will this new opportunity help make me a better stock trader?" If the answer is no, do not entertain it. **Boom Certified:** Learn the power of NO!!!

The last thing to consider when considering any investment opportunity is focusing on the facts vs hype. Questions you need to ask yourself are what exactly are the facts? What is the real opportunity? What are the solid numbers associated with this investment opportunity? If they are saying they do not currently have the numbers available for you to see, then why is this a good investment? Trust me, if the person bringing you the investment opportunities cannot clearly explain it to you and just wants you to trust the relationship, then please refrain or proceed with extreme caution.

Too good to be true stock investment opportunities usually present themselves on potential penny stock/pink sheet transactions. I have honestly been sucked in myself through great marketing regarding a new penny stock opportunity on more than one occasion. I have had some major positive returns on a couple like NIO, but I have also had some that have bombed. We will focus more on these types of stocks in the intermediate course, but I did want to mention it now because it aligns with this topic or section.

What facts would a good stock trader focus on before making a trade with a specific company? Companies:

- $ **Revenue**: Does the business have cash flow?
- $ **Debt**: Does the business owe a lot of Vendors/Investors/Others?
- $ **Margins:** Gross/Net - Is the business making a positive profit?
- $ **Alpha/Beta**: Is the stock risky?
- $ **Volume**: Trading Volume - Are there enough stock investors trading the stock?
- $ **52 Week High/Low**: Where is the current stock price in relation to this number?

I would not recommend you invest in any stock before looking at this basic fundamental information for a company/stock. Keep in mind, you could look at all the above information and Wall Street investors sell the stock because the company/stock has fallen out of favor for any number of reasons. Maybe it is just too sensible and not the new stock pick available at the time. Just be thoughtful about making stock selections and stick to your rules to do what you can to avoid buyer's remorse after the fact.

Now that we have discussed Greed, let us switch our focus to Fear. What is FEAR after all? **Boom Certified:** False Evidence Appearing Real! We do not have to struggle to remember at the top of 2020 when the Coronavirus was taking hold worldwide and shelter in place orders were given. Industries were closed overnight (i.e. restaurants, bars, nightclubs, airlines, cruise ships, hotels, and mail/retail stores). I can remember the fear that hit me, my family, and my friends during that time period. The news was reporting the COVID-19 infection cases rising and that we might be required to shelter in place for months. The stock market dropped double digit percentages from early February 2020. With everyone panicking the big four-letter word set in... FEAR! I can remember wondering how far the market would fall. I talked to several stock traders that were scared of the potential fall and sold out of stock positions, and even took losses on stocks.

What did I do? Nothing, no sells, at all...at the end of February. Once March hit, I was in wait and see mode, and working on a plan to identify undervalued stocks. The past is prologue! The market has recovered from every market downturn since the Great Depression! If we can recover from that collapse, then we can recover from anything. We will do an in-depth review regarding market crashes in the intermediate course, but I wanted to explain how and why I developed this mindset while everyone else was panicking.

This leads me to my first and main rule to managing fear as a new stock trader...**Boom Certified:** Do not panic! Stay calm. You can make better decisions when you are calm compared to when you are excited and scared. Rule #2: Do not sell! Remember you have not experienced a loss until you sell the actual stock. Any time before that moment, you proceed with a sell, you have the opportunity for the stock to appreciate and recover. Rule #3: Remember why you purchased these companies and stocks in the first place. Did the company or stock fundamentally change because of the market crash or correction? If the answer is no, and it was a fluke occurrence, then you wait it out. The US market has a proven track record of recovery.

Lastly, I will leave you with the words of Warren Buffet, "Be greedy when everyone is fearful, and be fearful when everyone is greedy!" I have learned to live by these words for several years and it has really helped me in my life, in and outside of the stock market.

WHAT IS WINNING TO YOU?

What does winning look like for you? If I asked a room full of Pivot Point Investor members, I am sure I would get a variety of responses. This question is a part of personal goal setting, but you are drilling down to an entirely new level. I believe your number #1 pursuit should be to become a profitable Day or Swing-Trader within your first 60-90 days of active trading. Profitable is described to be any amount that is more than the investment bankroll you started with. If you start with $500 to invest/trade, then $501 is profitable trading. There is a simple explanation...the stock market does not move in a straight line. You will experience market volatility, but do not be alarmed. Remember volatility is the understanding that changes can occur rapidly and unpredictably.

Once you get to profitability, as a new trader, then you may want to focus on a specific dollar amount that you would like to make each day you trade. For example, a $100 per day trading goal, is in my opinion, quite reasonable and realistic. Remember you will not make this $100 every day that you trade, however you can average that amount over the course of a week of consistent trading or even a month. The key is consistency, discipline, and focus on obtaining your goal. One idea I recommend for new traders, is to complete a Vision Board. You might laugh at this thought, but positive visualization has been proven to work for people in all walks of life. Go to the internet and look for nice pictures for what you want your home office to look like. What kind of computer screen set up do you want to have? Do you want to wake up and log into your computer while in your pajamas? You may have laughed again, but if someone is switching from Corporate America to becoming a trader/entrepreneur full-time, the thought of never having to dress up again in a shirt and tie or dress may be motivation enough. Again, these are just suggestions to consider. What do you have to lose by trying 1-2 or all the suggestions, until you come up with the formula that fits you best?

The last thing to consider when creating your winning blueprint, is networking, and finding a mentor to help you navigate the crazy stock market world. I know that networking is not natural for a lot of people. It takes guts to go to events or hop on chat lines and converse with people that are most times total strangers. I remember being a new insurance agent as well as a financial advisor and going out to meet people. Networking felt strange at first. I have always been a people person, but there is a real art to networking that I now understand now that I did not fully appreciate when I was getting started. One thing I now know, is you do not have to talk to every person at the event. If it is an in-person event, you can arrive and scan the room. Does anyone look familiar? What is your reason for being at the event? More often than not, I would say focus on meeting likeminded people that are interested and involved as active stock traders. What style of trading do they focus on? Do you have to force the conversation or is the person easy to talk to? These questions may seem simple and straightforward, but they can really help you focus on your "why" for the event.

While networking or participating in online sessions, consider identifying a person you would consider serving as a mentor. What characteristics should they have? Some of you may be thinking...a mentor, I am an introvert or an independent person, but everyone needs support. I highly recommend you consider seeking out a trading mentor as soon as you are on the patch to actively trade. A mentor is simply a person who already does what you want to do and has some level of success with whatever the job or skill you would like to acquire. A lot of times mentors are older, but they do not necessarily have to be. Sometimes a trader may be more comfortable with having the same sex as a mentor, but that should not be a requirement in my opinion. I will say all my prior mentors except 1 have been men, but that was not something I was focused on finding. I was looking for whoever was competent, available for my questions, and friendly. Give some thought to what you would like to see in a personal mentor and put yourself in situations to be able to meet and then identify that person. Once you find your mentor, be impeccable with your word, listen, and ask questions. Do not assume anything until you have mastered your chosen trading style, and even then, stay coachable. Remember, arguably the greatest basketball player of all-time, Michael Jordan, still had a coach. Mentors are like coaches in some ways. They can often see things we cannot see about ourselves and give a different perspective regarding trading and life in general. Your mentor may just make a suggestion that breaks you out of a two (2) week slump that had you in the red, but now you are rebounding!

Closing

Thank you for traveling this journey with me. It is my hope that as you turned the pages, you found the tools needed to ensure your success as a trader, coupled with the confidence needed to win through development of your customized strategies for financial gains.

BOOM CERTIFIED BIG IDEAS

- What is happening in the world influences what happens with your trade!
- Knowledge is key to financial gain.
- It is not a loss or gain, for you, as a trader, until the stock is sold!
- Knowledge is power. Do your homework!
- Your attention to detail influences your bottom line, and it starts with taking care of you.
- Learn the Power of NO!
- Do not panic. Stay calm!

ABOUT THE AUTHOR

JD Boom is a proud Alumnus of Morehouse College. He is an Independent Financial Advisor with 20 years in Banking, Insurance, Real Estate Investing, and the Financial Services industries. He has worked at several fortune 500 companies inclusive of Progressive Insurance, Merrill Lynch, and New York Life. JD Boom is a Swing Trader who utilizes Fundamental Strategies as his stock picking foundation. When he is not dissecting companies and developing new stock investment strategies, he enjoys spending time with his four children, sandy beaches, and beautiful ocean views.

Made in United States
Troutdale, OR
11/03/2026

56845119R00056